NEEDl

MW00779966

FOR
BEGINNERS

ARI YOSHINOBU

© Copyright 2020 - All rights reserved.

The content contained within this book may not be reproduced, duplicated or transmitted without direct written permission from the author or the publisher.

Under no circumstances will any blame or legal responsibility be held against the publisher, or author, for any damages, reparation, or monetary loss due to the information contained within this book, either directly or indirectly.

Legal Notice:

This book is copyright protected. It is only for personal use. You cannot amend, distribute, sell, use, quote or paraphrase any part, or the content within this book, without the consent of the author or publisher.

Disclaimer Notice:

Please note the information contained within this document is for educational and entertainment purposes only. All effort has been executed to present accurate, up to date, reliable, complete information. No warranties of any kind are declared or implied. Readers acknowledge that the author is not engaged in the rendering of legal, financial, medical or professional advice. The content within this book has been derived from various sources. Please consult a licensed professional before attempting any techniques outlined in this book.

By reading this document, the reader agrees that under no circumstances is the author responsible for any losses, direct or indirect, that are incurred as a result of the use of the information contained within this document, including, but not limited to, errors, omissions, or inaccuracies.

Table of Contents

Introduction

Crafting is a great way to keep yourself busy and be productive in your downtime. You can also make homemade gifts if you are good at a craft. But it can be hard to find a craft that interests you, is not too hard to learn, and does not require a lot of supplies to get started. Making a major investment to learn a craft is a lot to ask if you do not even know that you will be good at it or enjoy it!

Luckily, needle felting is a craft that is easy to learn and does not require a lot of supplies. This book will give you an overview of the supplies that you need to get started, as well as what you might want to invest in to step up your game after you learn the process.

There are also step-by-step instructions that will help you learn the basics. You will get a chance to try your hand at several different designs, starting with flat designs and progressing to three-dimensional (3D) sculptures.

Once you understand the basic process, you will have no problem creating your own projects. Wait until you see how easy needle felting can be, and how cute the final products look! You will love making these items for yourself, your family and others.

Chapter 1:

Needle Felting

Felting is a way to make wool or cotton into a piece of fabric by connecting the individual fibers. This is one of the few ways of creating fabric that does not involve weaving or spinning. Felting changes the texture of the wool and allows you to do more with it than you could with just the loose fibers. There are many ways of felting, including knitting a project and then felting, wet felting, dry felting, and needle felting.

Needle felting might sound like a very involved process that involves various machines, but it is a project that you can do easily by hand. Needle felting allows you to create 3D objects from a piece of cotton or wool. Using a barbed needle, you work the fibers of the fabric so that they bond together and feel solid. This is a very hands-on craft that enables you to transform loose fiber into a picture that you have in your mind.

After you make the cute designs from this book, you will understand how the texture can be worked into shapes, and you will be able to create your own ideas from scratch. The basic techniques of needle felting are easy to learn and, as you work through the provided patterns, you will start to create your own patterns.

What is Needle Felting?

Basically, needle felting is a method by which to compress loose fibers into a single fabric. This means that you are tangling fibers into a matted piece somewhat like the matted fur sometimes found on long haired pets or the proverbial rat's nest of tangled hair, only needle felting is cleaner and way more fun!

As you start matting a piece of fabric, you can decide what you want to create from it. Since all felting starts as agitating fibers into a tangle, you can start working while you let your imagination run wild. You can keep your project on a flat surface as you needle felt and make flat designs. Just because your felting project is flat does not mean it has to be a square or rectangle sheet! Using cookie cutters and stencils, you can make flat felt projects of different shapes.

You can then take those flat fabrics and shape them into different 3D sculptures. While you are felting, you can also easily shape the fibers to make them look like certain characters or objects. Needle felting sculptures of animals is really popular, and you will learn to make plenty of them in this book.

A perk of needle felting is that you can also use this method to mend clothes! You can use flat felted fabrics as patches on clothes. Once you understand how needle felting works, you might even feel confident enough to use this skill to repair your sweaters and socks!

A Brief History of Needle Felting

In the mid-1970s, Eleanor Stanwood learned to shear the sheep that she was raising in Vermont. By the 1980s, wool was a less popular textile since cotton is much more versatile. Cotton is cheaper to buy, can be made into anything, and is machine washable. In the interest of not wasting wool, Stanwood started turning the fibers into batting before wet felting the material to add layers to bed comforters. After experimenting with a needle punching machine, Stanwood found that she could make scarves, and even sturdier 3D designs. She started using this technique to make jewelry. Stanwood sings the praises of needle felting because the jewelry it makes is biodegradable and can be composted.

Other fiber artists learned this technique and needle felting grew in popularity. To name a few:

Ayala Talpai, inspired by Stanwood, wrote the first book on needle felting: *The felting needle—From factory to fantasy*. Talpai has also written a needle felting workbook and leads workshops in the community and in public schools. Talpai has supported herself as an artist by selling her needle felting crafts at local markets and making wedding garments.

Kay Petal makes needle felted dolls of famous people, and many celebrities have commissioned her work! Petal won her first award for a needle felted Albert Einstein doll less than a year after she started practicing. She said, "I never knew I was artistic until I started needle felting," which should inspire you to try this craft regardless of your previous experience—or lack thereof!

Sara Renzulli is known for her posable needle felted animal sculptures, and teaches workshops on the craft. Her website,

Sarafina Fiber Art, includes access to tutorials, videos for beginners, and online workshops.

Other Types of Felting

Needle felting is a great hands-on craft, but while you are learning about needle felting, you might want to know a brief overview of other kinds of felting as well. The goal of all the different types of felting is to turn loose wool fibers, also called roving, into a cohesive fabric. This fabric can be flat, and used to make other garments or works of arts. This fabric can also be 3D, and shaped into sculptures, statues, and stuffed animals.

Wet Felting

Wet felting is a process that uses water, soap, wool, friction, and pressure to turn loose wool fibers into felt fabric. The soap and water act together to open up the fibers so that they easily catch onto each other. The movement of your hands or a textured surface against the soapy wet wool creates friction, which helps to push the fibers together and makes them become matted and tangled. Like needle felting, wet felting can be used to create flat or three-dimensional objects.

Wet felting can make thick sheets of fabric that can be sewn together into complete garments. This is a nice way to make wool clothing without having to learn to knit or crochet! You will get the heft, warmth, and look of wool without having to weave the yarn fibers together.

You do not have to make sheets of fabric with the wool felting process. Other ways of wool felting create fabrics that look completely different than how you usually picture wool!

Cobweb Felting

Cobweb felting is a method that makes a lightweight felted fabric with a 'cobwebby' texture. Instead of making a thick sheet of felted wool, cobweb felting makes a light and airy fabric with more thin than thick areas. There might even be stylish holes in places!

Instead of using a needle to tangle the roving together, you start cobweb felting by gently pulling the roving apart. The fibers will just barely stay attached to each other, but you will be pulling fibers apart to make thin areas and gaps. You will thin the wool roving until it is about twenty-five percent longer and twenty-five percent wider than you want your scarf to be. Wet felting will cause the fibers to shrink.

After you get the wool roving pulled thin, completely wet it with a spray bottle that has a few drops of soap added, and then start to agitate the fibers with your hands. You can also roll the fabric up in bubble wrap or another bumpy, flexible surface. After a lot of agitation, you can give your fabric a pinch test. You pinch it between your thumb and first finger, and pull up. If the fibers stay together, you have felted it enough. If the roving pulls apart, then you need to add a bit of water and keep working the fibers.

When you unroll your fiber, you wad it up and drop it on the table over and over again. This helps the fibers to adhere to each other so that they start to become a fabric. At this point, you will notice that the fibers have shrunk and puckered. After you wash out the soap and let it dry, you will have a cobweb felted piece of fabric.

Lattice Felting

Lattice felting is a wet wool felting technique which produces a fabric that has holes deliberately added into it. This is because to make the fabric, you will lay out the wool roving in a lattice pattern, almost like a loose weave, and felt the wool with the holes in place.

Like with cobweb felting, you will need to thin your wool roving out before you make a lattice design. Thinner wool actually makes the felting process easier because it will get completely wet which makes it easier to agitate the fibers.

First you lay out the thin pieces of wool roving all in one direction. Then you take more thin strips of wool roving and put them on top of the first layer but in the opposite direction. This creates the lattice pattern that looks like weaving. You can keep the design straight or you can make it look more haphazard and artsy.

Spray the wool roving generously with a spray bottle of water that has a few drops of soap added. Create friction on the fibers by working them with your hands. You can also use bubble wrap or a bumpy surface, just as you did for the cobweb felting. After felting the fibers a bit, wet them again so that they are completely saturated.

You will repeatedly drop your fabric just as you would for cobweb felting. Remember, this process makes the fibers shrink and harden and that completes the felting process. Do the pinch test once again, making sure that the fibers stay together when you try to pull them up. Rinse the soap out, let the piece dry, and enjoy your unique lattice felt fabric.

Felt Fabric

Felt is a fabric that comes in various shapes, sheets, and rolls. Most people are very familiar with felt because it is used in childhood crafts and is often the first fabric on which people sew. It is a thick and sturdy fabric, but the felt that you are familiar with is most likely synthetic. There is nothing wrong with using synthetic fiber in crafts, and your project will turn out nicely if you use synthetic wool or cotton in needle felting. The main difference is the textures. Pure wool and cotton feel softer and slightly springy, whereas synthetic fibers feel more dense.

Felting Knitted Goods

Sometimes knitters felt their finished products by using hot water in the washing machine to agitate their fibers. Needle felting is similar, except you are using a needle to work the fibers instead of hot water. Also, you do not have to knit the initial product! If you are a knitter, you will enjoy having another craft to do with your wool, but you do not need to be a knitter—or crafty in any way—to learn and enjoy needle felting.

While felting a complete knitted product changes the texture of the item, needle felting gives you more freedom with your design. After you create the texture, you can shape the wool into anything you want!

Tips and Tricks

This list of tips and tricks can help you before you get started needle felting. Keep these in mind while you learn. This book includes step-by-step processes for each craft, so the important tips will be restated in the relevant sections.

Make It Firm

Keeping pieces firm is a key part to creating a successful 3D needle felting project. Since the wool fibers are soft, they will spring back when you press them in, but the overall felted piece will be firm.

Roll It Tightly

One of the beginning steps of most projects is to roll loose wool felting into a ball or cylinder before you use a needle on the fibers. The tighter you roll the wool fibers, the easier it will be to complete your project because the core of your sculpture will already be firm.

Tie a Knot

Another way to get a tight, firm core is to tie a knot in the center of your fibers before you start to roll it up.

Make Short Motions

Needle felting requires you to make short stabbing motions into the wool. You do not need to stab the needle all the way through the wool and into your foam pad work station.

Rotate the Piece

As you are needle felting a piece of wool, make sure you keep rotating the piece while you work. If you keep turning the wool, you will be sure to evenly felt the material. Keeping your work in motion will also keep "dimples" from making your final product look uneven.

Start with Less

While many patterns will tell you how much wool roving to use for each step, it is always a good idea to start with less. You cannot take wool away from your project once you start felting it, but you can easily add more fiber which can help your piece get bigger and thicker.

Your Shape Will Shrink

After you have fully felted your fibers, the finished product will be about thirty percent smaller than what you started with. This is the ideal change in size, but note that if you overwork your felting and make it as hard as a rock, it will be over seventy-five percent smaller than what you started with! And super hefty on top of that!

Keep Your Needle Straight

Keep your needle straight when you work: straight into the fibers, straight back out of the fibers. Pulling it out at the same angle you pushed it in will prevent your needle from breaking. If you twist or bend your needle while it is tangled in the fibers, the tip will break off, and you cannot safely continue felting wool if there is a sharp needle embedded in it.

Be Patient

Learning a new skill takes time, and needle felting is no exception. Since you are making stabbing motions with a sharp barbed needle, you will want to be incredibly careful with your work, even if this means starting slow.

You might get frustrated because, as you are working on it, your project does not look like you think it should. The wool roving mostly looks like a mess of fiber, even if you have felted it into a smooth shape. It is not until the final steps of a project when you are putting everything together that you will finally be able to tell your hard work has paid off.

Practice Makes Perfect

The projects in this book will take you step-by-step through the needle felting process. They will provide you with the instruction that you need as you learn general needle crafting skills and discover how they can all work together to make beautiful and adorable projects. That being said, finishing this book will not make you a master fiber artist. There is nothing wrong with practicing the same craft from this book multiple times before moving on to the next. Even if you go through every project once, coming back through to do them all again will be great practice and will definitely improve your needle felting skills. Hopefully the projects in this book will also serve as jumping off points and inspire you to create your own patterns!

Chapter 2:

Needle Felting Equipment

Recently needle felting has become a very popular craft because it is so easy to learn. It does not hurt that the finished product is very cute! To get started with needle felting, you will need some basic equipment.

Basic Equipment

This basic equipment is a must-have to begin needle felting. You will also learn about some different tools and textiles that you might want to try after you complete a few practice projects.

1. Notched Needle

You need a special needle to complete needle felting crafts. Notched needles are the standard tool used. Notched needles have been used as far back as 1859, when they were used in needle punch machines to make batting for blankets. These needles have small notches, or barbs, along the shaft and tip. These barbs grab the fibers when you stick the needle into the wool, tangle it up, and leave it stuck in your shape even as you pull the needle back out. The more you poke the fibers with the notched needle, the stiffer it will become.

To get started with needle felting, you can use a standard notched needle and easily complete the basic crafts. There are four different types of felting needles you might want to use as you become more skilled, but any notched needle will work nicely for beginners.

Felting needles are sharp, so you will want to be careful and pay close attention to your finger placement as you work. Although not a basic supply, finger shields are available if you are worried about stabbing yourself. These are like flexible rubber thimbles that you can wear over your fingers to protect them from the needle. Since they are rubber, they will still allow you a range of movement as you work.

2. Unspun Wool Fleece

Unspun wool fleece can be found in two styles: roving and batts. Roving means the fibers have been brushed to all run in the same direction so that they are smooth. Batts are sheets of thick wool that have fibers going in all different directions.

Both roving and batts can be used for needle felting. For a beginner, batts are easier because the fibers are already somewhat tangled. You will be able to needle felt a bit and quickly see how the process works and get an idea of what your final product will look like.

3. High Density Foam

High density foam is necessary for your work area when needle felting. Since the needles poke through the wool, they can not hit a hard surface or they will break. You also do not want to use a standard pillow or cushion, because you will get holes in it. Using high density foam will protect your needle from breaking while also preventing needle damage to work surfaces.

Felting Needles

Felting needles are sturdy, and are made to tangle wool fibers into something more firm. Still, you must be considerate when working with your needle. Make sure to always pull it back out at the angle you pushed it in so that you will not break the tip of your needle. This will ensure that your needles last longer, and will also keep you from getting hurt. If the tip of a needle has broken off into your wool, you will either have to extract it—very carefully!—or scrap the entire piece and start again.

Felting needles come in a variety of styles and lengths. They also have different numbers and positions of notches, or barbs, on the shaft of the needle. These notches are what agitate the wool when you stick in your needle, so the number that you have will affect how much work you will have to do to get the wool to the desired texture.

To begin a felting project, you will want to use longer and thicker needles because they will go further into the wool. This, along with innumerable notches on the shaft, will help the needle to catch and tangle more fibers.

Once your wool is tangled, it will be harder to push the thick needle into the fibers. At this point, you can switch to a finer needle so that the work will not be hard, but you will still be able to create texture and volume in your fibers.

Needles with delicate tips have notches close to the point. These are used to smooth out your project when you are on the final steps. This will also make your project look less fuzzy. On the other hand, if you want your sculpture to look fuzzy, there are needles that will give it that appearance.

1. Triangle

Triangle needles have three sides or edges.

2. Star

Star needles have four sides or edges.

3. Twisted/Spiral

Twisted or spiral needles are actually triangular in shape, but they feature a twisted blade to agitate the wool fibers in different ways than the triangle and star needles.

4. Reverse

Reverse needles are the type that will make your finished product look fuzzier. These needles have opposite notches that pull fibers out of your work to make it look fuzzy and fluffy.

Once you see some of the projects that you will be making, you will understand why some sculptures might benefit from a fluffy finish.

Needle Gauges

Felting needles come in different gauges, typically 32, 36, 38, 40, and 42 gauge. Needles with low numbers are thicker, and can be used on coarse wool and to get your projects started. Needles with higher number gauges are thinner, which means that you can use them once your wool fibers are tangled or when you need to do more detailed work.

Felting Needle Pens

Felting needle pens are not for writing—they are tools that hold up to three needles at once. Using multiple needles at the same time makes the felting process incredibly efficient. Once you become more confident with needle felting, you can even create your own version of this tool by combining several needles together. You can attach them with string, wire, or hot glue.

These pens have a sturdy grip attached so you can hold them firmly. Many needle felting pens also have a protective plastic case around the needles. This case gets pushed up when you are working and comes back down automatically when you pull back from the fiber.

Another tool that you might be interested in trying that is called a "clover tool." This tool can hold one, two, or three needles while you work. A benefit to using this tool over a premade felting needle pen is that you can change out the needles. While thicker needles are used at the beginning of a project to quickly agitate more fibers, you will need to use thinner needles as the project progresses. If you are using a felting needle pen, you will need to stop using the pen at a certain point and start to use a more delicate needle. But the clover tool allows you to change out needles so that you can use the tool until you get to the final detail work of your project.

Keep in mind that felting needle pens and homemade tools that use multiple needles are best used at the start of a project. The multiple needles will make quick work of a large flat piece, the body of an animal, or the foundation of a sculpture. As you get into more detailed work, you will need to work with just one needle, and eventually use a higher gauge needle to finish it off.

Best Needle for Needle Felting

As you become a more skilled needle felter, you will be able to choose from a variety of needles according to your craft level, your project, and the stage of your work. For beginners, a 38 gauge needle in the best choice. Within that gauge, you can pick either a spiral or triangular needle. This standard needle will help you to complete the projects in this book as well as many that you, yourself, will create. Pick a needle with a high number of notches because this will make your work more efficient. As a beginner, it is rewarding to be able to see the fruits of your labor quickly, instead of doing a lot of work with a less notched needle and getting frustrated at the lack of progress.

If you purchase a needle felting kit, it might come with a variety of needles. Even if you do not get an entire kit, you can buy a pack of needles—this is an affordable option which not only provides you with different needles but replacements for

19

broken needles. Unfortunately, you will probably break a few no matter how careful you are with your work. The notches on the needles will also wear off over a long period of usage, rendering them ineffective.

Needle Felting Wool

There are many different fibers that you can use for needle felting. Most crafters use wool from sheep, but other fibers, such as those from other animals, plants, and even synthetic fibers, also work well. Even wool from sheep comes in a lot of varieties, depending on the breed of sheep from which the wool is shorn. Breeds include Merino, Icelandic, Wensleydale, Shetland, Romney, New Zealand, Corriedale, Norwegian Lincoln, Herdwick and more. Each of these wools have different textures that you will learn about later. Different textures mean that they will work differently with the notched needles.

Wool is described with microns, with the higher micron rating the coarseness of the fibers. How coarse the natural fibers are will impact how much you will have to work the fibers to adequately felt them. Once it is shorn from the animal, wool can be processed in different ways. These processes might also affect how the fibers can be felted. Over time, you will work with different fibers and discover which ones work best for your style.

1. Short Fiber Wool

Short fiber wool is the best type of textile to use as a beginning needle felter. Since the fibers are short, they are easier to work into a fabric. Since the fibers are coarse and uncombed, this is the best wool to use for the center of your sculptures—it is actually sometimes called "core wool." The coarse fibers work into a sturdy core that will support the additional felted elements that you add to your projects.

Short fiber wool is cheaper than finer wool, which is another plus for beginning crafters! It can be tough to sink a lot of money into a hobby you are not sure you will enjoy, so using short fiber wool to get started is an affordable option.

Short fiber wool comes in a batt, a loose sheet, or a roving. Batts or loose sheets are most likely the easiest way to get started with needle felting, as the roving is a loose rope that some might find intimidating.

2. Long Fiber Wool

Long fiber wool comes combed so the fibers are all running in the same direction. It will look smooth when you purchase it. You can use this for needle felting projects without much trouble, but it is not the best choice for beginners. Since long fiber wool is so smooth, it takes a lot more needle agitation to get the fibers tangled together. It will take more time and effort to get these fibers felted, and that can be discouraging for beginners.

Because long fiber wool is so smooth and is high quality, it is a great fiber to use for more advanced needle felting projects. It comes in a variety of natural and dyed colors, so it is the optimal choice for special projects that you want to use as showpieces, sell, or give as gifts.

3. Wool From Different Breeds of Sheep

Wool from different breeds of sheep felts differently, so you must consider what type of wool you need for your project before you get your supplies.

Merino

Merino wool has a fine-medium texture, so it will take more work to properly felt. Once it is done, your project will look smooth.

Icelandic

Icelandic wool is coarse and hairy. Keep in mind that the undercoat felts better than the outer coat.

Wensleydale

Wensleydale wool is unique because it has wavy fleece. This is a great wool to use for animals with long hair, or if you are felting a person or a doll with curly hair.

Shetland

Shetland wool is medium-coarse, but some of the coarse fibers are incredibly difficult to felt. You may wish to wait until you have more experience before using this wool.

Romney

Romney wool is medium-coarse and therefore ideal for needle felting. Some Romney wool is also very soft, so it can be a good option for making stuffed animals or dolls.

New Zealand

New Zealand wool is medium-coarse so it is great for needle felting projects. It is easy to use, but the finish will not look as smooth as a Merino wool project will look.

Corriedale

Corriedale wool is also medium-coarse, so it is a great wool to use as you get started with needle felting.

Norwegian Lincoln

Norwegian Lincoln wool is medium-coarse, so it is an ideal option for needle felting. This type of wool is more coarse than Merino wool and Corriedale wool, if you are caught trying to decide between the three.

Herdwick

Herdwick wool is incredibly coarse, so it is a good wool to use for felting projects.

4. Wool From Other Animals

For unique needle felting projects, consider using wool from other animals. Alpacas, llamas, camels, angora goats, and rabbits all produce fibers that you can use for needle felting. You can even use fur from your pet dogs and cats if you integrate it into other fibers!

Alpacas

The younger the alpaca, the softer the fiber. Texture and length also depend on the part of the alpaca from which the fur is gathered. The blanket fur comes from the main part of the body, between the hind end and neck. This fiber is long and soft. Fur from the neck and upper legs is soft but short, while fiber from the lower legs and belly is fairly coarse.

Llamas

Llama fibers are very soft and delicate. Llamas do not produce much wool, so this rare fiber is rarely used for needle felting.

Camels

Camel fiber is very soft, with tiny natural curls in the texture. When mixed with other wools, the camel fibers will stand out and make a pattern.

Goats

Fiber from angora goats is called mohair and is very shiny. Kid mohair is soft and curly. Yearling fur is more coarse, and wavy instead of curly. This fiber is rated at about 20 microns, meaning that it is fairly soft, though it gets coarser with age.

Rabbits

Angora rabbits also produce soft fur that can be used for needle felting.

Best Wool for Needle Felting

With so many different wool fibers available for crafting, you will want to consider what is best for needle felting. Fine wool is softer to work with, but will take much more time and effort to felt into an attractive sculpture or project. Coarse wool is easier to agitate with notched needles, so you will be able to see the results of your work quickly.

There are wools that are medium-coarse, which is a good middle ground between fine and coarse wool. Medium-coarse wool fibers are easy for the notched needle to grab and agitate, but your final product will still have a smooth finish.

To complete the projects in this book, you will only need a few colors of medium-coarse wool. However, if you want to have a lot of colors on hand so that your creativity can run wild, it is possible to buy kits that have small bundles of many different colors.

Additional Supplies

These supplies are not at all necessary for needle felting. Even the most professional fiber artists might not use these tools, but they are options worth knowing about, because they do influence your work and change how your projects can look.

ARI YOSHINOBU

Carding Brushes

Carding brushes are wire brushes with fine bristles that can be used to smooth and mix wool roving. Hand carders are brushes on a long handle, so you can keep a better grip on them as you work with your fibers. In a pinch, you can use clean pet brushes, because the wire bristles are about the same quality.

Carding brushes use the wire "teeth" to grip fibers that you want to merge together. You use two of these brushes at once, with one color of wool roving in the bristles of one brush, and another color of wool roving in the bristles of the other brush. You gently combine these hand carders so that the wools blend together. This will give you natural highlights in your wool. It is also a great way to get variegated colors of wool roving for certain needle felting projects.

Once the wool has been successfully combined, you can carefully extract it from the bristles of the hand carders and use it just as you would any other wool roving.

Fabric Shavers

You might think that fabric shavers are just for getting pills off of your sweaters and winter coats, but they work wonders in providing the finishing touches on many needle felted items. When you finish a piece of needle felting, you might have some fibers still sticking out of your item. This might be a good look, if you are creating a furry animal! But if you want a smooth felted ball to make stylish jewelry, then you can trim these pesky fibers with a small fabric shaver to give your craft a smooth, sophisticated finish.

26

Chapter 3:

Getting Started

Learning the basics of needle felting will set you up for success with future projects. If you have never done needle felting before, this is the perfect first project for you. If you have tried needle felting, this is a great project to practice your skills and get in the right mindset for the more involved projects that will come later.

To get started, you will try the basic movements of needle felting to make a heart.

Materials Required

1. One or two felting needles

2. Wool fiber (red color)

3. Foam cushion (for base)

4. Straight pins

Steps to Follow

1. Take your red wool and tear a thick sheet of it. Hold the edges of the roving and pull so you are tearing from the center. Make sure what you tear off is at least ½ inch more than your planned size, because the fibers are longer than your finished, matted project will be. You will always need more wool fiber than you think you will because the fibers get tangled up and become shorter.

2. Lay the torn wool on the foam to start working on it. Be considerate of what you are using as a base for your needle felting. You can use a regular cushion as a base, but you will end up with a lot of holes in it! Foam cushions are firmer so they provide a sturdy work space, while still allowing the needles to get into the foundation to best agitate the wool.

3. Poke the wool with your needle all over. Poke any random spot you see. Just start poking at the wool. If the wool fibers still look fairly smooth, you need to work on them some more. Get the fibers very tangled before moving on to the next step.

4. Use the straight pins to outline the shape of the heart. This is so you can see what shape the felting needs to be; outline it in the way that works best for you.

5. Tuck the excess wool into the middle of the shape, and work it again with the felting needle. Poke it all over so the fibers get tangled together to hold this heart shape.

6. Compress the center of the shape. You want to make sure it will hold together on its own.

7. Fold the excess wool in the center. Agitate the fibers so they grab each other to hold tight.

8. When you turn over the heart, you will see a bunch of fuzzies from where your needle poked through the wool into your foam mat. You can work to gently needle felt these fibers back into the opposite side of the heart. This will smooth it out.

Look at your sweet red heart! Your first basic shape is ready. You have needle felted your first project, and now you know the process.

Chapter 4:

Advancing Your Shape

After making the flat heart shape, you understand the basics of how needle felting works, and how it feels to tangle the fibers together and create shapes that hold together. In this chapter, you will learn how to create advanced shapes. You will needle felt different parts that will be put together to create a sculpture.

You will also learn the concept of using different color wools. Different elements of the sculpture will be different colors, and you will combine the colors and parts to make one cohesive sculpture.

For this needle felting practice, you will be following a step-by-step process to make this adorable cartoon character.

Materials Required

1. Felting needles

2. Different colors of wool

3. Foam base

Steps to Follow

1. First, rip off a piece of wool. Remember to make sure that it is slightly bigger than you want your sculpture to be. This first piece of wool is for the body of the sculpture, so you want to get enough wool to make a firm core.

2. Use this wool to create the body of the sculpture. Agitate the wool until it is firm. Keep rolling more wool into the body in even layers so that it will be sturdy.

3. Next, you will create the belly of the character. Take a bit of the white wool and felt it into an oval shape. Keep this somewhat flat, because you will be sticking it onto the body that you have already created. The white wool is more to give definition to the character than to give it more volume. When you get the white wool into a nice oval shape, use your needle to felt it onto the body.

4. The next step is to create the eyes with small pieces of black wool. You will just need a tiny bit of black fibers for this step, and you will carefully felt it into small circles. Be very aware of your fingers as you work on this small scale!

If you do not feel confident enough in your felting skills to work with something so small, you can cut little circles of flat black felt to use as eyes. Just be aware that synthetic sheets of felt are most likely shinier than the wool you are using for the rest of your sculpture. This will make your character's eyes look different than the rest of your hand made craft.

After you have your eyes, carefully attach them to your character's head by using your notched needle to tangle the fibers together.

5. Your character needs some ears! Take more of the wool that you used for the body, and felt two ear shapes. Leave a bit of stray wool hanging from the ears so you can use your notched needle to push these fibers into your character's head to attach them.

6. Last, but not least, your character needs feet to stand on. Use the same color of wool that you used for the body—or if you want your character to wear shoes, pick another color to use.

Felt thick egg shapes for the feet, and make them firm enough so that you can sculpt them by hand. It might take more agitation than you have used previously, so keep working. Pause every so often to test the texture of the feet. Once you can mold them into shapes, you can flatten the bottom side of it so your character will be able to stand. Make the feet or shoes look however you would like.

Add some wool fiber to the top of the shoes or feet, and felt a little of it into the shoes. Leave some to felt back into the body of your character so that it can stand on its own two feet!

You have made your first sculpture! Now you have got down all of the basic skills needed for needle felting, so you are ready to progress to the next level.

Chapter 5:

Skill Improvement

You have now made a flat needle felted shape and a 3D sculpture. Although the method of making a sculpture is quite different from making a flat shape, all of the basic skills are the same. You make the same motions with the needle whether your product is flat or 3D. Even attaching pieces to a sculpture body involves the same needle movements.

In needle felting, your end result is highly dependent on which material you use and how you use it. There are a few things to take into consideration while needle felting, as these factors will affect your workflow. They will make you more efficient, improve your performance, and elevate the quality of your work.

Improve Your Needle

For the first two projects, only a standard notched needle was needed. However, to be more efficient, you can use a needle felting pen, or create your own version by attaching two or three needles together. Every time you insert them into the wool, they will be working double or triple time for you!

Using different gauges of needles will also help to step up your needle felting game. Thicker needles are great for starting projects, whether you use them alone or as a needle felting pen. But the more you work the fibers, the finer of a needle you will need to be able to make a difference in the felting. Using a more delicate needle will also prevent your needle tip from breaking off when it is forced in.

Using a reverse needle is also a fun way to change up your felting style. Remember, this is the needle that has notches that are the opposite of what the standard needles have. When you use the reverse needle, you will pull out bits of fiber to make your final product look fluffy or fuzzy. This can be a really cute effect to use on animal sculptures!

Vary Your Fiber

So many different types of fiber were defined in Chapter 2 that you should have an idea of what types you might like to work with. There are a variety of coarse fibers that are good for beginners. Medium-coarse fibers will also be easy for beginners to work with.

To step up your needle felting game, try working with medium-fine wools like Merino. Wensleydale is also a great fiber to try, since it is naturally wavy. You can needle felt the ends of some Wensleydale wool into a felted horse sculpture for a flowing mane and tail. You can felt it on the head of a doll or person sculpture for gorgeous locks. Once you experiment with different fibers, your imagination will run wild and help you to figure out what you can create from scratch, or how you can embellish existing patterns.

Incorporate Stitching

You can incorporate stitching on your needle felting projects, whether they are flat or 3D designs.

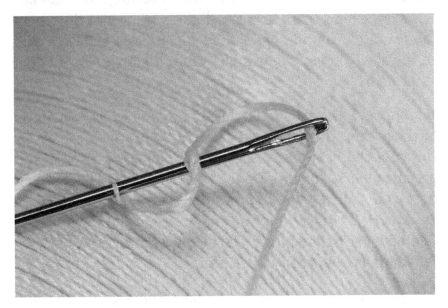

Embroidering Flat Felted Designs

When you are embroidering flat felted designs, you can either stitch directly on the felted wool, or you can put the whole design on a piece of fabric to make a wall hanging or to incorporate into a quilt or larger piece of fabric art.

To make a felted design on fabric, you will felt a flat design just as you did with the heart in Chapter 3. It can be any shape that you choose. Instead of working directly on your foam base surface, put a piece of fabric between your felting project and your foam base. Felting on top of the fabric means your felted design will become attached to the fabric "canvas"! The wool fibers you are felting will become tangled with the fabric. Since the fabric is tightly woven, its fibers will not come loose, but instead will tightly hold the felted material.

Once your felted design has adhered to the fabric, you can add accent colors with embroidery thread by sewing loose stitches around the felted part. You can also add stitches to the empty fabric around your design. For example, if you felted a moon in the sky, you could stitch stars into the area surrounding your moon.

If you have created a flat felted design without a fabric backing, then you can stitch right on the finished project. If this was the heart project from Chapter 3, you could add accent stitches directly onto the heart to make it look broken. Just as if you were outlining your fabric-backed design with embroidery, you will want to keep your stitches loose on the felting. If you tighten the thread too much, it might cause your felted wool to bunch or lose its shape.

Also keep in mind the fact that your stitches go through the entire project, and will be seen on the opposite side of the design. Normally, there is a "bad side" in sewing where all the ends of stitches can be hidden away in a garment's hem, on the inside of work, or beneath the frame. Adding stitches to a flat felting that is meant to stay flat and not mounted to anything means that both sides of the design are visible. There is a way to make the stitching work on both sides, and you can tuck in and trim any loose ends.

Embroidering 3D Felted Designs

You can add stitches to 3D felted designs to give more detail to your work. For example, for the cartoon character you made in Chapter 4, you felted small black eyes to add to the face. If you did not feel comfortable using a felting needle for such small-scale work, you could cut felt circles and attach them to your character's head. However, another option would be to use thread and stitch eyes onto your sculpture. Using embroidery is a great way to level up your needle felted sculptures.

When embroidering a 3D object, you will need to be careful about how deep your needle goes. You will want to keep your stitches shallow and loose so that they do not pull apart the fibers that you have previously felted. If you felted your project to completion, it should be pretty firm, so it will hold stitches well.

Keep in mind that most embroidery thread has a sheen to it. Your felted elements will look soft and fuzzy, but any embroidered accents will be shiny and crisp. This can work well for a project and add a lot of interest, but you will want to take it into consideration in the planning stages. If your finished product would look harsh and surreal with crisp elements added on, you do not want to go through the trouble of adding them and potentially ruining what you have created.

Use Wires and Other Supplies

You can use wire, stuffing, batting, and other supplies to help build your needle felted sculptures.

Wires

There are several ways that you can use wires to your advantage when needle felting. First, you will need to consider the different types of wire, specifically sculpting wire and covered wire. Wires can be used to build a skeleton for your sculptures. They can also streamline your work process so that you have fewer steps necessary to complete your design.

Sculpting Wire

Instead of using short fiber wool as a core for all of your projects, you can use wire to form a base. Think about this step as you are planning your pattern so that you can save on wool. Using wire to form an animal's body will not only save your money and wool, but it will also cut down on the steps needed to complete the project. Instead of having to needle felt a solid ball for the core, you can shape wire and then add layers of felting over it.

There are different gauges of sculpting wire you can use. Thicker wire might require a tool to cut it into the lengths you need, and again to shape it. But this thicker wire will hold its shape, and also be sturdy if you are making a sculpture that will have many layers of felting and additional elements on it. Using thick wire also means your final product will be more durable, so it can be carefully handled and moved around without losing its core structure.

Thinner wire can be cut with regular scissors and is easy to twist into shapes. However, since it is thin and delicate, too many layers of felted wool might weigh it down and push the wire out of the intended shape. If you are doing a light project that will not be handled or moved around too much, thinner wire is a great way to create a skeleton foundation. Thinner wire is also one way to keep limbs slender and proportionate. Instead of having to felt a dense piece of wool for an animal's appendage, you can use wire as the base and just add a light layer of felting over it to keep the visual on point.

This wire can also add flexibility to your project. Needle felter Sara Renzulli is known for her posable needle felted animal sculptures. On her website Sarafina Fiber Art, she has tutorials for how you can use wire to make your animal and people sculptures flexible.

If you are unable to find the exact gauge of wire that you need, consider getting creative and making your own! You can twist together two thinner gauges of wire to make a slightly thicker option. You can even mix a thin and thick gauge of wire together to make a sturdy yet flexible wire skeleton option for your sculpture.

Covered Wire

Covered wire can be used for projects if you need the structure of wire, but do not cover the wire with needle felting. Pipe cleaners are one example of covered wire. They can give your sculpture a sturdy base, because they are strong and flexible. As an added bonus, pipe cleaners are already covered in fuzzy fibers, so they will fit the look of your project.

Pipe cleaners are thin wires twisted together with chenille fibers. They come in a variety of types and lengths. Most pipe cleaners are thin, with bristly chenille fibers sticking out all around the wires. There are also incredibly soft and fluffy chenille pipe cleaners that will be a great addition to luxurious sculptures you might be creating. The wire of these pipe cleaners are typically the same gauge as the thinner kind, but the fibers are longer to give the illusion of fluffiness.

Pipe cleaners come in thicknesses of 4, 6, 9, and 12 mm. Keep in mind that this references the thickness of the fibers, which will impact the overall look, or fluffiness, or your project. This thickness does not refer to the gauge of the wire at the core.

You can find pipe cleaners in a variety of colors, including some that have glitter or metallic accent fibers added in with the chenille. There are also bump pipe cleaners, where the stem will be relatively thin and then fluff up into a larger bump shape on the stem, then go back down to thin. This type of pipe cleaner can be used to add interesting features to your needle felted sculptures!

In addition to pipe cleaners, there are also brands of wire that are covered in fabric or a thin layer of paper. These are smooth wires, compared to the fuzziness of pipe cleaners. For this type of wire, the gauge does refer to the wire itself, since the layer of fabric or paper covering it is very thin. These wires are typically available in 22-, 26-, and 32- gauge.

Covered wire, such as pipe cleaners or fabric covered wire, can also be used as decorative elements in your statues. If your sculpture is a basket, you can braid natural-colored covered wire together to make the woven handle. If your sculpture is holding a bouquet of flowers, you can use green pipe cleaners or green fabric covered wire as the flower stems. Using covered wire in these ways will not only cut down the number of steps in your craft project, but will make it look more polished overall. Making green felt stems will take a lot of small scale needle felting, and it might not look right once you are done. The felted stems would have to be very dense to stand up straight, and the weight of such a bouquet might topple your sculpture! Using green covered wire will prevent your flowers from drooping.

Stuffing

Just as you can use wire to create a structural foundation, you can use stuffing to round out your 3D figures. Stuffing is less expensive than wool fibers, so using rolled up bits of stuffing instead of wool fibers for the core of your sculpture will save you money. It also reserves your wool fibers for bits of the craft that will be seen, instead of hiding the higher quality materials inside of the sculpture. You can even needle felt the cotton or synthetic fibers so that they will be more tangled together, and therefore create a stronger, denser core for your sculpture.

If you are making stuffed animals instead of sculptures, using pillow stuffing at the center of your project will keep it cuddly. If you need something firmer but still soft, you can try quilt batting. The options are limitless, so use your imagination!

Use Cookie Cutters

You can make any flat shape you choose by using straight pins to map out the area you will be felting. If you want to practice set shapes, you can also use cookie cutters. Keep them flat on your foam base and put the wool inside of the cookie cutter. Keep felting it to the edges of the cookie cutter, just as you did with the straight pins.

Cookie cutters are a great option because you have so many choices available to you. If you want to make flat felt shapes, pendants, decorations, or ornaments for a certain holiday, you can just buy a set of cookie cutters! Craft and baking stores will have sets like this available, so you can buy a set of assorted winter shapes, Christmas shapes, Valentines shapes, Thanksgiving shapes, and more.

Cookie cutters also come in general shapes like circles, squares, stars, lightning bolts, and more. Using these cookie cutters will give you the ability to needle felt a variety of shapes that you can then morph into other shapes or even sculptures. You can needle felt a rectangle and a circle and then combine them to make a microphone. You can then leave this as it is, add a hanger so it can be an ornament or a decoration, or make it a pendant for a necklace. You can even felt it onto a piece of fabric and add stitching like explained above.

Or you can take the flat rectangle and add fibers to it until you have made a cylinder. Likewise, you can add fibers to the circle shape until it is a ball, and you can felt it to the cylinder to make a 3D microphone.

Using cookie cutters to make shapes is a great way to practice your needle felting skills, but it is also a good way to find inspiration. Mindlessly making shapes within the borders of a cookie cutter might help you to see some of the things that you could make.

Chapter 6:

Beads

This chapter will give you step-by-step instructions to create beads using needle felting techniques. As Eleanor Stanwood, one of the first needle felting artists, said, using needle felting for jewelry is ideal because wool is a renewable resource, the beads are biodegradable, and they can be composted! Instead of spending money on fast fashion jewelry, making your own needle felted beads is an environmentally friendly way to make unique jewelry.

Materials Required

1. Needles

2. Merino wool

3. Foam base

4. Warm water and dishwashing soap

Steps to Follow

1. Mix together the warm water and a squirt of dishwashing soap.

2. Take two tufts of 4 to 5 inches of wool. This much wool will make a bead that is about the size of a small cherry. If you want to make many beads that are all the same size, you might want to consider weighing the tufts so you can ensure your beads will be uniform.

To start with, you will want to choose two tufts of the same wool. Once you see how the bead comes together, you can experiment by choosing two different colors of wool. This will make your bead to have two colors swirled together.

3. Roll one of the tufts of wool very tightly.

4. Place the tightly rolled tuft at a right angle to the bottom of the other tuft.

5. Roll them up together very tightly, starting from the bottom, until you have a rough ball shape.

6. Hold the roll together very tightly, and dip it into the soapy water for a few seconds.

7. Hold the ball in the palm of your hand and add a drop of soap to it.

8. Put the ball between your palms and start to roll it. Do not apply pressure to the ball, as it is malleable in this state and applying pressure will change the shape. You are simply rolling the fibers together, not condensing them into a denser ball.

Once the ball starts to shrink and harden, you can apply a little more pressure to it as you are rolling. This will help it shrink into a felt bead.

9. Rinse the soap off of the bead and let the bead dry. Once it is dry, you can poke a needle through it to make a hole, or thread a needle through it if you know you are going to put it on a string.

The bead will be pretty dense and firm, but since it is made of wool, it will be a little springy and squeezable. Felt beads are slightly fluffy, but you can use a shaver for removing sweater pilling to give it a smoother finish.

You have made a felted bead! This process is called wet felting, and while it is different from needle felting, it is still a hands-on craft. Using soap and water will make the bead firmer when it dries. This method could also be used as part of the process of needle felting a more involved sculpture. Adding soap and water to the body or core of a statue would make it dense and sturdy so that other more traditional needle felting elements may be attached.

Now that you have learned this style of felting, you can experiment with the process and make more beads. Having rolled two tufts of fiber together to create a bead, you can make unique beads. You can also experiment with sizes, using smaller tufts of wool for smaller beads, or larger tufts to make large beads.

After feeling the texture of this first bead, you can change how much pressure you apply to the bead when you are rolling it between your hands. You can apply pressure in different areas of the bead. You could make a long bead by rolling it back and forth in one direction, instead of rolling it all around. Wait until it starts to take shape with the soap and pull out fibers from the ends, making it slightly pointy at each end. When the bead is almost done, you can press each side against a flat, hard surface to make a cube or rectangle. You can flatten your bead into a disc by either applying a great deal of pressure with your hands, or use a hammer to press it flat.

You can embellish the finished bead. Consider using stitching, as was discussed in Chapter 5. You can wrap the beads in wire to give them a caged look, which is very popular in statement necklaces. You can even anchor small beads, sequins, or pearls to the felted beads to completely transform their appearance.

Think of what you would like to make with these felted beads, and that will influence the size that you need to create. You can make enough beads to string together on a necklace or bracelet. You can use the beads like a single charm on a necklace or bracelet. These also make cute key rings and cell phone charms. You can even thread them on a long string and hang them around your house like a garland, or hang them from the ceiling like a mobile. Your designs and jewelry do not have to be made only of felted beads, either. You can alternate jewelry beads with felted beads, use twists of colored wire, or use gold and silver elements to make unique designs that spotlight your felted beads.

Chapter 7:

Mini Teacup Pincushion

You have been using straight pins to outline shapes for flat needle felting projects, but where have you been keeping these pins? This adorable mini teacup pincushion is the perfect way to practice your needle felting while making a practical item to use for your craft supplies. This step-by-step guide will teach you how to make this cute teacup pincushion.

Materials Required

1. 20 grams of Merino wool roving

2. Separate small amounts of Merino wool in different colors for cup decorations and the beverage that will be in the teacup

3. Two 40 gauge triangular needles

4. Foam base

Steps to Follow

1. Take a length of wool roving that measures about 50 x 4 centimeters. This will become your teacup, so use the wool

that you have the most of, and make sure it is one that will allow the embellishment colors to show up nicely.

2. Tease it out gently so that it can lay out to make a flat strip.

3. Roll it up to make a short tube.

4. Use needles to start shaping it like a teacup. Using two needles, or a needle felting pen, will make this step of the process go much quicker. As you are shaping the cup, make sure that you are not just making it a round cylinder. Think of how a teacup looks, and try to squeeze in the bottom of the piece that you are working on. This will give your teacup a smaller base, and will make it look more realistic and delicate.

5. When you have formed the teacup, take a pinch of wool to make a little handle. Remember, this should be the same color as the wool fiber you used to make the teacup so it will form together to make one cohesive item.

6. Shape the bit of wool on your foam first. Think of what a teacup handle looks like and try to mimic that shape. It might be a little difficult since you are working with such a small bit of wool, but the handle can be solid. It does not need to look like a real teacup handle you can put your finger through—those details can be added with embroidery thread before you finalize your project.

While it is still soft, attach your needle felted handle to the cup. Simply felt the loose ends of the handle into the body of the cup.

7. Use one needle to give the handle a fancy shape. Poking the needle into a concentrated area will help stiffen it up and give it a more refined shape than the rest of the handle. This shape can look like a little loop or scroll at the bottom of the handle,

like you might see on fine china. It adds a touch of whimsy to your teacup.

8. Cover the cup with a thin layer of wool. This will help it look smoother, and more like the finish on a teacup (minus the china's sheen) instead of leaving it looking like raw needle felting. Use one needle to finish the surface to achieve the maximum smoothness.

9. Tear off a good bit of wool for the beverage color. Since this is a teacup, you will want to use colors that look like teas, coffee, or hot chocolate.

10. Place the beverage colored wool on top of the cup. Needle felt it into place by winding the wool in a circular direction as you work. This will make it look like a liquid beverage swirling in a cup.

11. Add some surface patterns to the cup itself with different colors of wool. Using pinks, reds, and greens would be a cute way to imply a design of flowers and leaves. You can also simply make patterns of dots or stripes. Keep the needle felting work of this step loose and free, so the fibers will closely resemble hand painted china.

In addition to felting designs on the cup, you could embellish it with beads, gems, or pearls. You could also use embroidery thread to hand stitch designs on the cup instead of needle felting them.

While you are embellishing the cup, use a complimentary color of thread to add stitching along the edge of the handle. This will function like an optical illusion to give details to your handle and make it look more like something you can grab to drink from, instead of looking like a solid handle piece.

12. To make a matching saucer, gently tear a length of roving that measures about 30 x 4 centimeters.

13. Wind it into a circular saucer shape. Begin working on it with both needles so this process will go much quicker. As you needle felt the saucer, continually turn it in your hands so it will get worked into a quality circle. Pinch the edge between your thumb and finger as you work, because this will give your saucer a slightly raised rim and help make it look realistic.

Once your saucer is big enough to compliment your teacup, or about 8 centimeters in diameter, then you need to cover it with a fine layer of wool, just like you did for the teacup. Remember, this will make the saucer look smooth and refined instead of showing the tangle of the felting.

To finish off the saucer, you can needle felt a design that matches the cup, or even just add a simple stitch around the edge like you did with the teacup handle.

Your mini teacup pincushion is ready. You might think that it is so adorable that it would make a good toy, too. Many children would probably love to have a felted teacup for their own tea parties. You could even use this project as a basic pattern, and continue making an entire tea set!

Chapter 8:

Needle Felt Writing

This chapter will give you a step-by-step, in-depth guide to needle felt your name onto a pillow or cushion. Once you learn needle felt writing, you might like to practice by adding people's names to personalized items, or even making beautiful needle felted quotes to hang up as home decor.

Materials Required

1. Felting wool in one color.

Once you learn needle felt writing, you might be able to do variegated colors across the same word by carefully tucking in one color as you move on to the next. But to learn the basic skills of needle felt writing, it is best to just use one color.

2. Felting Needle

3. Sponge.

This sponge is replacing the foam base you usually use for needle felting projects. The sponge is small enough to fit inside the cushion cover, since you will want to needle felt on only one side of the cushion. If you do not have a sponge in place behind the cushion, your needles will go through both layers of the cover and felt the sides together so that it will be impossible to put over a cushion. As you work, periodically check the sponge to make sure it is still in the right place so that you are only going through one layer of fabric.

4. A cushion or pillowcase on which to felt.

You can felt onto a cushion that does not have a zipper to remove the cover, but you will have to be more aware of how deep your needles are going. If it is at all possible to remove the cushion cover, you will want to do so. You can always use a pillowcase for this practice.

Steps to Follow

1. First iron the pillowcase or cushion cover. If it has wrinkles, you might needle felt over these wrinkles and they will permanently be visible on the pillow. Or, worst case scenario, the wrinkles will pull out the needle felting writing as they ease out. Get your pillowcase ironed as smooth as you can.

2. Write your name on the cushion cover with the pencil. If you mess up, you can rub out the pencil markings or make sure it will be covered with your needle felting in the end. Try to mimic the style or font in which you want your name. If you want it to look like a cursive font, write it that way with a pencil. If you want it to be in all capital letters, write it that way. Making it look exactly how you want with the pencil will make it easier for you once you actually begin felting, because you can just follow your drawn lines.

3. Insert the sponge inside the cover behind the place where you wrote your name. This is the spot where you will be needle felting, and you do not want your needles to go through both layers of pillowcase. Pay close attention to the sponge to ensure it is always behind your work area.

4. Pull out a thin strand of wool from the ball of your chosen color.

5. Place the strand of wool over the first part of your pencil markings. Begin to stab it into the pillowcase with your needle.

6. As you move on to the next letter, add more wool onto your pencil markings. Make sure that your sponge is under your new work area. You will also want to make sure that you are using the same amount of wool for each letter, so it looks like one cohesive word.

6. You can use a needle holder or needle felting pen to use multiple needles at the same time. This will agitate the wool faster so that it will felt onto your pillowcase easily.

Your name is done! Now that you know how to needle felt letters, you can make other designs and decorations, and even try to use several different colors within the same project.

Chapter 9:

Ornaments

In this in-depth, step-by-step guide, you will learn how to create ornaments for the holidays—but you might just want to keep them up year-round and call them home decorations.

Materials Required

1. String that is thin enough to pull through dense felted balls

2. Scissors

3. Wooden beads

4. Embroidery needles

5. Felt balls or pom-poms, which call for wool, water, and liquid soap

Steps to Follow

1. Make felted balls or pom-poms. This part of the project involves the wet felting that we learned in Chapter 6. For these

steps, you will need wool in many colors, a small bowl of water, and a few drops of dishwashing soap.

2. Mix together the warm water and a squirt of dishwashing soap.

3. Take two tufts of 4 to 5 inches of wool. This much wool will make a ball that is about the size of a small cherry. For these ornaments, you will want to make many different sized balls, from small to large, in order to have a lot of different decorating options.

4. Roll one of the tufts of wool very tightly.

5. Place the tightly rolled tuft at a right angle to the bottom of the other tuft.

6. Roll them up together very tightly, starting from the bottom, until you have a rough ball shape.

7. Hold the roll together very tightly, and dip it into the soapy water for a few seconds.

8. Hold the ball in the palm of your hand and add a drop of soap to it.

9. Put the ball between your palms and start to roll it. Do not apply pressure to the ball, as it is malleable in this state and applying pressure will change the shape. You are simply rolling the fibers together, not condensing them into a denser ball.

10. As you are rolling the ball and it begins to firm up, you can apply pressure in different ways, and on different parts of the ball, in order to make it different shapes. Think of the shape of some of your favorite ornaments and try to recreate those shapes in your felted balls.

11. Rinse the soap off of the ball and let the balls dry.

12. As the balls dry, gather the rest of your necessary supplies.

13. Plan the overall look of your ornaments by laying them down in order in a straight line. This is the time to play with the design of the ornaments, and mix and match colors. You can make ornaments for specific holidays, or decorations to keep up for entire months or seasons.

You might want to use red and green felted balls to make Christmas ornaments, or blue, white, and grey felted balls for general winter decorations. Orange and black felted balls will look cute for Halloween decor, or you can use orange, yellow, and brown felted balls to make decorations that you can leave up for all of autumn. You can use pastel felted balls for spring, and add egg-shaped beads or pearls in between for extra decoration.

Adding in beads, wood, or other textured elements will make your ornaments and decorations incredibly unique. Play around with the designs and let your creativity guide your process.

14. Measure a string that is three inches longer than double the length of your ornament. Since your designs are laid out in front of you, it is easy to just hold up the string, then fold it back on itself to get double the length of the ornament.

Use a ruler or measuring tape to make sure that you are adding three inches onto that length of string. If you are in doubt, string up to two feet long will be more than enough for your ornament.

15. Insert one end of your string into the eye of your embroidery needle. Make sure you knot the end of the string. If you use a small knot, your first element might fall off of the

string. If you use a complimentary color of thread you can knot it around your first felted ball, and it will not be visible on your ornament. If you want to start with a decoration, you can tie a bead at the end of your string so it will ensure the ornaments will not fall off once you hold them upright.

16. Pass the needle through all the ornaments so the thread combines them all together.

17. Leave a loop above the top element of your ornament. This is how you will hang up your decoration.

18. Thread the string back through all of your felted balls and beads. This will give your ornament an extra sturdy string to hang from. Remember to cut your string so that it is double the length of your ornaments!

19. Tie another knot at the bottom of your ornament. Make sure that it will not pass back through the felted ball. Tie it back around the last bead or ball to be extra safe.

20. Trim off any extra string that is hanging from the final knot on your ornament.

Your ornament is ready to hang up! These are so cute, you may want to leave them up year-round. Although these ornaments are simple to make, they are attractive enough to attach to gifts. They will not only make your gifts look attractive, but your gift recipient will be able to hang the needle felted ornament in their own home—two gifts in one!

Chapter 10:

Cherry Bag Charms

It is hard to believe that this needle felting project is so quick and easy to make, because it looks adorable and professionally done! People will think you bought this purse charm, and will be astonished when you tell them that you made it yourself. In this chapter, you will learn how to create cherry bag charms with step-by-step instructions.

Materials Required

1. Felting wool (natural and red)

2. Felting needle

3. 8" length of leather cord

4. Metal key ring

5. Green felt

6. Foam base

7. Low-temperature hot glue gun

Steps to Follow

1. Fold your leather cord in half and hold it in the middle of the metal key ring.

2. Pull the ends of the leather cord through the loop and secure it into the ring. This will hold your leather cord tight to the metal key ring. You should not need to tie it. If you decide later that you want to take this charm off of the key ring, you can easily pull the leather cord back through the loop.

3. Tie a knot on each end of the leather. At this point, you should have the leather cord looped around the key ring, with two equal lengths of leather hanging down. There should be one knot at the end of each piece of leather cord hanging down.

4. Wrap a long length of the natural colored wool roving around your fingers. It should form a loose ball that is about the size of a golf ball. It will not be dense like a golf ball, though, because you need to make sure there is a hole in the center of the roving.

5. Slip one of the lengths of leather through the middle of the wool roving. You should see the knot sticking out of the end of the wool.

6. Use your hands to shape the natural colored wool into a tighter ball, and then needle felt it to make it as tangled as it can be. When you have finished felting the natural colored roving, it should, of course, be the size of a cherry.

7. To create a second cherry, wrap another long length of the natural colored wool roving around your fingers. Remember that it is a loose ball, about the size of a golf ball. Make sure there is a hole in the center of the roving.

8. Slip the other length of leather through the middle of the wool roving. The knot will be sticking out of the end of the wool.

9. Use your hands to shape the natural colored wool into a tighter ball, and then needle felt it to make it as tangled as it can be. When you have finished felting the natural colored roving, it should be the same size as the first cherry you made.

10. Add a thin layer of red wool fiber over each cherry. Use a needle to secure it onto the natural wool roving. Continue to needle felt the red wool fiber onto the natural colored cherry until it is firmly adhered to the surface. At this stage, it should look like you have two cherries on brown stems, hanging from a key ring. But you are not done yet!

11. Use the green felt to cut out two leaves. If you want to use green wool roving to felt leaves yourself, you can. However, with the leaves being so small, needle felting them yourself would not cause them to look much different than using green felt. The choice is up to you!

Whether you cut leaves from a sheet of green felt or needle felt your own leaves, you will need to hot glue them to the back of your cherry stems. You can loosen the leather loop, hot glue the leaves on, and then tighten the leather loop back over the ends of the leaves. This will not only cover the hot glue, but will provide a little extra security against your leaves falling off.

You have made the cutest cherry purse charm! Now that you see how fun and easy these are to make, you can make many more pairs to spruce up all of your bags and give to friends.

Chapter 11:

Mini Needle Felt Owls

You previously made an animal when you made a cartoon character as your first 3D project in Chapter Four. Hopefully you loved making animals, because in this fun project, you will learn how to create three unique miniature needle felted owls. You will not believe how cute these creatures are!

Materials Required

1. Felting Needles

2. Foam base

3. Low-temperature hot glue gun

4. Wool roving in grey, white, teal, and light teal

5. 2 black beads for eyes for each owl, up to 6 total

6. Foam eggs, one for each owl's body (You can buy these from a craft shop, or shape your own from larger blocks of foam or styrofoam)

Steps to Follow

Owl Option #1

1. Wrap the grey roving around the foam egg. Use the felting needle to poke the wool into the foam repeatedly. Keep agitating the wool fibers until the felt is smooth.

2. Working on the foam base, use the light teal wool roving to create a heart shape. This was the first project that you learned to do in Chapter 3, so you might need to refer back to those instructions. Remember that you can shape a heart by using straight pins as an outline, or even by using a heart-shaped cookie cutter as your border. If you are using straight pins as a border, you might consider leaving them in place if you want to make all three versions of the owl, because you will be making a heart shape again.

After agitating the light teal felt into a firm heart shape, make sure that the felt is smooth.

3. Place the light teal heart shape on the grey body. Poke the heart shape into the grey felt over and over until it is smooth and adheres completely to the egg shape.

4. Take the small black beads and use your low-temperature glue gun to stick each bead into place on the owl's heart-shaped face.

5. Now is the time to customize your owl! You can use embroidery thread to stitch on a little teal beak below your owl's eyes. You can also use the teal thread to make little stitches on your owl's chest that will look like feathers.

Owl Option #2

This foundation for this owl will be created much like the first owl was made, but other elements will be used to make this creature look unique.

1. Wrap the light teal roving around the foam egg. Use the felting needle to poke the wool into the foam repeatedly. Keep agitating the wool fibers until the felt is smooth.

2. Using the foam base as your work station, take a length of white wool roving and tangle it into an oval. This will be a cute white belly for your owl, so after you felt it a bit, hold it up to your light teal felted egg and make sure the size looks right for a belly.

If you need to make it larger, you can add more white wool fibers while you are felting. If your white belly oval is too large, start folding in some of the excess fibers around the edge. Working from the edge towards the center will help you to keep the oval shape, but will also make it smaller.

3. Place the white felted oval onto the light teal egg-shaped body. Make sure that you get it into the perfect position, and needle felt the white oval onto the egg.

4. Working again on the foam base, use the teal wool roving to create a heart shape. This is how you made the face for your first owl back in Chapter 3, so you can refer back to those instructions if you need to. You can shape a heart the same way you did for your first owl: by using straight pins as an outline or a heart-shaped cookie cutter as your border.

After agitating the teal felt into a firm heart shape, make sure that the felt is smooth.

5. Place the teal heart shape on top of the white belly. Depending on the size of your white oval, you might need to have the teal heart overlapping from the white oval onto the grey body.

Poke the heart shape into the white felt (and grey felt, if necessary) over and over until it is smooth and adheres completely to the belly and egg shape.

6. Take the small black beads and use your low-temperature glue gun to stick each bead into place on the owl's heart-shaped face.

7. Now you can further customize your second owl! You can use embroidery thread to stitch on a little beak below your owl's eyes. Consider using grey thread for this owl's beak, since the face is made of the vibrant teal. Use the teal thread to make little stitches on your owl's white belly to look like feathers.

Owl Option #3

This foundation for this owl will be created much like that of the first owl, but other elements will be used to make this creature look unique. This is the most involved owl design, so save it until last as will you have practiced your skills with the first two owls.

1. Wrap the grey roving around the foam egg. Use the felting needle to poke the wool into the foam repeatedly. Keep agitating the wool fibers until the felt is smooth.

2. Using the foam base as your work station, take a length of white wool roving and tangle it into an oval. This will be a cute white belly for your owl, so after you felt it a bit, hold it up to your grey felted egg to make sure that the size looks right for a belly.

64

If you need to make it larger, you can add more white wool fibers in while you are felting. If your white belly oval is too large, start folding in some of the excess fibers around the edge. Working from the edge in will help you keep the oval shape, but will work to make it smaller in the process.

3. Place the white felted oval onto the grey egg-shaped body. Make sure that you get it into the perfect position, and needle felt the white oval onto the egg.

4. Use a long strip of light teal wool roving and keep working on your foam base. Felt the strip so it makes a somewhat thick length of rope. Hold it up to your owl and see if the light teal rope can completely outline the white belly. You need it to be this long, and then add in a bit extra length for this owl's unique beak.

5. Once your light teal rope of needle felting is long enough, needle felt it all around the white belly as a border. Start from the top, and needle felt it into place in a clockwise direction. When you get back to the top of the owl's head, you should still have a bit of the light teal felt left. Go straight down the owl's forehead to make a beak. Work the remaining bit of the light teal roving into a flat circle on the owl's face.

6. Take the small black beads and use your low-temperature glue gun to stick each bead into place on the owl's face, putting one on each side of the light teal felting nose.

7. Now you can further customize your owl! You can use light teal embroidery thread to make little stitches on your owl's white chest to look like feathers.

Your owls are ready. It is incredible how different the same base project looks with just a few tweaks or even alternate colors of wool. You can use these three owls to make cute woodland scenes as decorations or tablescapes.

Chapter 12:

Button Making

While most of the projects you have learned so far have been cute decorations, this chapter will teach you how to make something very practical! With step-by-step instructions, you will learn how to create a button using needle felting.

Materials Required

1. Felting needle

2. Wool roving, any color

3. Embroidery thread, color matching your roving

4. Foam base

Steps to Follow

1. Take a piece of wool roving in your choice of color. Loosely shape it into a flat disc about 2 centimeters thick.

2. Round out your roving and fold it in from the edges so that it has a diameter of about 5 centimeters.

3. Agitate the wool fibers with your notched needles. Felt the button until it has tightened up to be about a third of the size you started with.

4. As you felt the button, hold the edges between your thumb and first finger. This will create a slight rim on the edge of the button. Leave the cup shape in the middle. Even if it seems like a deep cup, it will equal out when you add the finishing touches.

5. Keep felting the button until it has reduced down to your desired size.

6. Using a standard needle, poke four holes in the center of your button. You do not want to use a felting needle for this step, because the notches will pull out some fibers from the holes. Having loose fibers around the button holes will make it difficult to see the holes to sew on your button.

7. Now you can use this craft as a button on clothing, make it into jewelry and pins, or wear it as a brooch.

This button has a diameter of 3.5 centimeters, with a thickness of 1.5 centimeters. Once you see the finished size of this button, you can make more buttons at this size, to keep them uniform for a garment, or you can try to make some even smaller, depending on the item of clothing on which you want to add buttons. To make smaller buttons, you can use a bit less wool roving, or simply felt the fibers even more tightly so that they will stay together.

If you use this pattern to make buttons for clothes, remember to hand wash these garments. Washing the buttons in hot water or in a washing machine will wet felt the wool, making the buttons shrink up and get even firmer!

Chapter 13:

Felted Ball Earrings

In this chapter, you will learn how to create stylish felted ball earrings.

Materials Required

1. Felting needles

2. Wool roving in at least three different colors

3. Jewelry pliers

4. Large needles

5. Jewelry wire

6. Two earring hooks

7. Foam base

8. Bowl of water

9. Liquid dishwashing soap

Steps to Follow

1. Mix together the warm water and a squirt of dishwashing soap.

2. Take two tufts of 4 to 5 inches of wool. This much wool will make a bead that is about the size of a small cherry.

3. Roll one of the tufts of wool very tightly.

4. Place the tightly rolled tuft at a right angle to the bottom of the other tuft.

5. Roll them up together very tightly, starting from the bottom, until you have a rough ball shape.

6. Hold the roll together very tightly, and dip it into the soapy water for a few seconds.

7. Hold the ball in the palm of your hand and add a drop of soap to it.

8. Put the ball between your palms and start to roll it. Do not apply pressure to the ball, as it is malleable in this state and applying pressure will change the shape. You are simply rolling the fibers together, not condensing them into a denser ball.

Once the ball starts to shrink and harden, you can apply a little more pressure to it as you are rolling. This will help it shrink into a felt bead.

9. Rinse the soap off of the bead and let the bead dry. Once it is dry, you can poke a needle through it to make a hole, or thread a needle through it if you know you are going to put it on a string.

The bead will be pretty dense and firm, but since it is made of wool, it will be a little springy and squeezable. Felt beads are slightly fluffy, but you can use a shaver for removing sweater pilling to give it a smoother finish.

10. Repeat steps 1 through 9 until you have six beads made. You should have two beads of each color so you can make a matching set of earrings.

11. Take the jewelry wire and thread it through the eye of your large needle. You need to fold up the end of the wire so the balls do not fall off when you hold it upright. You can fold the wire into a small, square, or hammer it down to a flat base, like the head of a nail.

12. Lay out your felted balls in the order you want them on your earrings. This might mean that you let them dangle from smallest down to largest. You might have a preference on color order. Laying out your designs first gives you a chance to imagine how they will look as completed earrings, so this is your chance to test out every option.

13. Push the needle and jewelry wire through the first felted ball. If you want to add beads or other embellishments between each felted ball, make sure to add it here.

14. Push the needle and jewelry wire through the second felted ball. If you added beads or other embellishments after the first felted ball, make sure to add one here.

15. Push the needle and jewelry wire through the third and final felted ball. If you added beads or other embellishments between the other two felted balls, make sure to add one here before you finish off your earrings.

16. If you want to add more length to your earrings, you can leave extra wire at the top so the felted balls will dangle lower.

17. After you have decided how long you want your earrings to be, attach the earring hook at the end. Fold the wire over and twist it back on itself so the earring hook is secured and will not slip loose.

18. Trim off any remaining wire.

19. Repeat steps 11 through 18 until you have completed your second earring.

You have now made a pair of needle felted earrings. Add this to any jewelry you previously made with felted balls, and you are well on your way to being a jewelry designer!

The basic skills that you have learned by making felted balls and using jewelry wire and earring hooks will set you on a great path to continue making more jewelry. With these patterns alone you can make matching jewelry sets of felted ball bracelets, necklaces, and now dangling earrings.

Chapter 14:

A Mouse With a Sweet Tooth

Mice are not a fan of cheese. I know, I was just as shocked as you. This myth of mice and cheese has existed for a long time, but no one really knows where it originated from. Cheese offers no nutritional value to mice. Thus, in real life, cheese should not be given to mice, particularly pet mice. Although mice will eat cheese if it is available to them (they will eat anything if it is available to them), in reality, they have more of a sweet tooth! Thankfully, this little figure is not real—even if it looks real—and can have all the cheese its little heart desires!

In these mouse instructions, there is something called a Zullitool. This is basically a wooden wand that works wonders! It has a slight butter knife shape with a rounded handle that is much smaller. You do not necessarily need to have this tool to complete this mouse figure—I have a few alternatives which I will mention below—but it is helpful. Also, this tool is great for not just one project, but you can keep it in your needle felting tool bag to use to make all sorts of shapes. The Zullitool is designed to help you make shapes quickly and consistently. To me, this sounds super helpful! It also saves your felting surface because you are making shapes on the tool versus felting onto a pad. If you are interested in purchasing one, do some Internet searches to find some available. While you are there, watch a few videos to give you a good idea of how to properly use the tool. If you do not feel like purchasing the tool, you can also use basically any skewer, pencil, or use the handle of your multi-needle tool in the same way that I am going to describe in the instructions. Just be sure to remove the needles from the tool so that you do not injure yourself! However, for this project, a pencil will probably work the best.

Mouse Instructions

Materials

- Zullitool
- Felting needles

- Felting wool (white, pink, and black)

- Felting pad

- Small skewer (chopstick size works)

Steps

1. Start by taking out your white or off-white wool. Section off a piece that is about 8 inches long. This first piece is going to form the core of your little mouse.

2. Take this 8 inch long piece of wool and divide it into four equal pieces along the length.

3. Take your Zullitool and begin wrapping the wool around it. Start with one corner of one of your quarter wool pieces and wrap it around the smaller end of your tool. Wrap tightly and consistently. This end of the Zullitool has a pointed end. Start wrapping just below the pointed end. Wrap two or three times, then angle the wool toward the pointed end. As you round the pointed end, angle the wool back to begin moving down the tool. Repeat this angle a couple of times. This pointed end is going to become the mouse head. By wrapping the wool repeatedly, you are creating a nice shape. Be sure to wrap tightly, holding only what wool you need to wrap once, then pulling more into the figure.

Pro-tip: When creating the head, your wool will want to slip down the tool. An easy way to avoid this is to use your non-wrapping hand to hold the wool on the tool in place. Your fingers create a sort of barrier that will help the wool stay in place.

4. You should use approximately one full quarter of wool for the head piece.

5. Take a second quarter of wool and begin forming the body. Start just below where the head stops and criss-cross your wool as you wind it around the tool. This section should take about two quarters of your wool. The head and body should be around the same size. As you criss-cross your wool, the gap between the head and body will close up. If it does not, push the body up slightly to meet the head before adding your second piece.

Pro-tip: If you are running out of wool very quickly before you get a good enough shape, chances are that you are not wrapping the wool tight enough around the tool. Never worry: this takes some practice to get used to it.

6. Take the fourth quarter of wool and begin wrapping it around the body of the mouse. Move up and cover the back of the head as well. This piece will help you join the two separate pieces together to create one tiny mouse!

7. Grab your needles and felt the wool together to make sure it is secure. Pay attention to the area where you started and ended your wool pieces.

8. Slide your wool off of the tool.

9. Take a look at the wool you just removed and decide where you want the head and body to be. There should be a natural curve already established from wrapping the wool. This is a good place to create that head and body divide.

10. When you decide where it should be, gently fold the two pieces to create a curve. Again, the wool should naturally be leaning one way over the other. Now stab it around from all directions along the neck to hold it in place. You

will know when it is ready when the head stays curled all on its own.

11. Take a strong needle (a 38 or 36 will work out well) to stab back on the bottom side of the nose to create an indent that will form the nose and mouth. This area will have a lot of give to it because it was just a simple wrap. Take your time to firm this area up. Create a fish hook style to form the mouth on the bottom side. Make sure you stay right in the center.

12. Take another 8 inch long wool and split it into four pieces. Then take one of those four pieces and cut this in half around the center so that you have two pieces approximately 4 inches long.

13. Take these two pieces and wrap them along the flat end of the Zullitool. You should be making approximately 1 inch rectangles here. Do not criss-cross when you wrap in this section. Instead, wrap the wool evenly on top of itself. You should be able to wrap the wool around at least two or three times here.

14. Slide those pieces off of the tool. Now you have two rectangular pieces that are going to become the thighs.

15. Take the rectangles one at a time and attach them to the body by felting. Let the back of the rectangle blend into the body of the mouse. The other end of the rectangle will have feet attached to them, so leave the as-is for right now.

16. Felt to keep blending the thighs onto the body and felt below to close up the bottom of the body wrap.

17. Now find your pale pink wool. Pull off a very thin strand and trim to approximately 6 inches. Make sure that the

strand is the same thickness up and down. Consistent thickness is key!

18. Find a small skewer.

19. Start about 3 inches back from the point of the skewer. Grab your pale pink wool and begin wrapping it along the skewer. Do not overlap the wool too much here: just enough to make sure there are no gaps between the wraps of your wool. If there are gaps between the wraps of the wool, the piece will not hold its shape when you slip it off of the skewers and we definitely do not want that! Again, make sure that you are pulling the wool tight and wrapping consistently up the skewer toward the pointed end.

20. Wrap the wool all the way to the pointed end, then begin to wrap backwards toward your starting point. If your wrap was not consistent, you will run out of wool. You can either stretch the remaining wool to cover what you are missing or you can begin again. It is vital that your wool stops and starts in the exact same place.

21. When you reach the starting and ending point, take the skewer between your hands and roll it vigorously. This will encourage the wool to bind to itself and keep its shape for the next step. Press firmly between the palms of your hands as you roll.

22. Slide the tail off of the skewer and pass over it with your needle a few times to make sure that it is secure.

23. Now pick up the tail from your felting pad and run it between your palms again to finish securing the wool together.

24. Take another thin strand of pale pink wool about the same 6 inches in length. Cut it in half to make two 3-inch pieces.

25. Take one of your 3-inch pieces and wrap it around the small skewer in one place. This will create a small seed shape. Do the same with the other 3-inch piece of wool.

26. Pull the seed shaped pieces off of your skewer: these will be your feet. Set them aside for a moment.

27. To make the ears, take two pieces of wool and place them on your felting pad. These pieces should be thin but not see through. Stack a few layers of wool on top of each other to create a good starting point. These pieces should look like 2-inch squares.

28. Take your needle and draw a circle that is approximately the size of a dime in the middle of these squares. This should create a circle that is bordered by loose wool.

29. Take the loose wool from the top of the circle and roll it down over the circle. Felt it into place then roll the sides into the circle, one side at a time. Felt those into place as well. All of this loose fiber should be pointing down. Leave the bottom loose and repeat for the second ear.

30. Smooth out the ears on both the front and backsides, still leaving the bottom edge loose for attachment. Check the size of the ears against your mouse head before moving on.

31. Here we are going to make a little pucker in the ear shape. Fold your ear like a taco and felt the bottom closed. Alternate from side to side to secure it properly. Here, you have the choice of how big you want to make your ear. Move the fold up or down to make the ears smaller

or larger. Once you close the pucker, you can trim off any excess wool.

32. Set the ears aside to make the very tiny nose. Stack thin layers of pink wool on top of each other to create a little quarter of an inch square.

33. Grab the tail. Felt the tail on the back of the mouse in between where the two thighs came together.

34. Grab the feet. Felt the feet one at a time onto the open fringe of the rectangular thigh that you created. Felt primarily on one end. Take a single needle and go over the other end of the foot to make sure the wrap closes up properly. It is best to start with a strong needle to secure the foot in place, then move to a finer needle to close up the wrap and smooth out the shape.

35. Now move onto the eyes. Due to the curved shape of the mouse, a closed eye looks super cute. Take a thin strand of black wool and felt a curved shape on the sides of the face.

36. Grab the ears. Find a nice space on the head behind the end of the eyes to attach the ears. There should be enough of a gap between where the eye ends and where the ear starts. Felt the loose end of the ear onto the head to secure it in place.

37. Take another thin strand of black wool to fill in the ridges of the mouth. You have already created the shape: now all you have to do is outline it!

38. Take the square for the nose and fold the sides in to create a point at the top of the shape. Try not to felt on the pad, but place the nose point side down on the mouse and felt directly on the mouse.

39. Now, you can leave the mouse this white color or you can decide to add some color to it by layering thin patches of colored wool (grey, brown, black, etc.) over top to create a nice branded top coat. If you do decide to do a color, start with the back and wrap horizontally to cover the entire body. Be sure not to cover any feet or ears!

40. Felt again to smooth out any bumps or fill in any holes.

Your mouse is now ready for a piece of cheese, or maybe not?

Pro-tip:

If ever there was a perfect figure to make even cuter, a mouse would be it. Consider changing up the overall style of this figure to make it seem more cartoonish. Add a bow or blushed cheeks. Consider making a family of mice in different shapes and sizes. Make a very plump mouse or a tiny meek mouse. This alteration can truly unlock your creativity.

You can also keep experimenting with accessories with this project. Try creating a block of cheese or give your new mice pets something sweet to nibble on: try berries or a piece of chocolate. Get creative!

Chapter 15:

Perfectly Cuddly Teddy Bear

Teddy bears are one of the most beloved stuffed creatures ever designed. Okay, perhaps that could just be my opinion; if you think about it, almost everyone has at least one teddy bear at some point in their life. Who could not want an adorable little teddy bear? Even some dogs and cats enjoy snuggling or playing with a squeaky teddy!

What I particularly love about teddy bears is that they make great gifts for people of all ages. Unlike most stuffed animals, teddy bears are given as gifts or prizes for people from young to old! How fun and lovable is that?

What is truly great about this teddy bear figure is that you can change up the size to whatever you want! Consider making a tiny figure as a quick project or a larger figure to really hone in your needle felting skills. In the instructions, I have listed brown wool as the material to use in this project. I chose the brown wool because it is a very common teddy bear color and closely resembles the color of actual bears: if you remember, one of the main goals of this book is to make realistic or semi-realistic little animals.

Teddy Bear Instructions

Materials

- Brown wool

- Hamanaka wool (Japanese curly wool)

- Felting needles

- Felting pad

- Plastic eyes and nose

- A red bow (size according to your bear)

- Metal wire

- Sharp scissors

Steps

1. As with most projects, the very first step is to make a head. Take a good chunk of brown wool and give it a circular shape. This head should be a decent size no matter the overall size of the project that you are making. Most teddy bears have a larger head which helps give them their super cute proportions.

2. Now take another chunk of wool and create a cylinder shaped body.

3. Next, we are going to focus on the arms and hands which will be one shape. Take a metal wire and give it a length of a hand. Twist this wire around itself to strengthen it.

4. Roll some wool around it until it becomes firm. Keep layering wool to achieve your desired level of thickness. Make sure to keep measuring it up to the body to check if the proportions work out.

5. Add some more loose wool and felt it until it is firm.

6. Create two hands of equal length and thickness. Do another proportion check before moving on.

7. To make the feet, follow the same instructions. Remember that the feet should be longer and thicker than the arms. Create a sort of mutton shape here to give dimension to the thigh and small feet. These should be one long shape.

8. Begin attaching the body parts to the torso. Start with the head. You may seal this attachment with loose wool to strengthen the figure.

9. Use some Hamanaka (Japanese wool) and felt it all around the head. Create a tight spiral starting at the top of the head and winding down. Felt as you spiral down the figure and continue winding the curly wool past the head and onto the body. Make sure it is as even and neat as you can possibly make it.

10. Go back up to the top of the head and add more curly wool to add more dimension to the head. Be sure to blend this wool evenly. When adding wool to the top of the head you can cut small strips of the curly wool and pull it partly in your hands. Do not pull it apart too much to avoid creating holes. Only add this extra wool from the top of the head to about the middle. We will add some dimension to the face later.

11. Mark out where you want the eyes and make small cuts with your sharp scissors. After cutting the holes, poke the inside of the holes to make sure that the extra curly wool you added is firmly attached to the main head base. Attach the plastic eyes and try not to forget the glue! Wipe up any excess glue that might have leaked out.

12. Grab your normal brown wool to make the muzzle. Felt it on your pad to make it nice and firm.

13. Attach the muzzle to the face right between the eyes. Your figure will look a little funky with the two different colors at the moment. Never fear: we will be adding dimension to the face soon.

14. Now find some of the Hamanaka wool. Cut short strips of this wool and attach them to the muzzle with a thin felting needle. A thin needle is important to create a seamless and smooth layer. It is helpful to start on one side and add this extra wool across the muzzle moving

from top to bottom. As you add the wool, trim the excess that might stick up or not fit with the shape of your muzzle. It is also helpful to pull your small strips apart slightly to loosen them up and make them easy to attach smoothly. Attach the wool in sections and make sure that the muzzle is completely covered. Make sure to trim any wool that might be covering the eyes. Fill in any holes or gaps as necessary.

15. Add one last strip of extra curly wool to the center of the muzzle going from side to side.

16. Trim any excess wool to make the face neat.

17. Take some of the curly wool and make small ears. Teddy bears usually have rounded ears—make these flat. Make two of equal size and thickness.

18. Attach the ears to the top sides of your bear's head. Create a slightly curved shape when you attach the ears. Add extra layers of curly wool to strengthen the attachment and to smooth out the figure. Make sure that you add wool to all sides of the attachment. Again, use a thin felting needle for this step.

19. Grab your needle to make the curved inside of the ear more pronounced. Poke repeatedly in this area to create the desired shape.

20. Now we will attach the nose to the muzzle. In this tutorial, I have listed a plastic nose. You can attach this nose in the same way as the eyes. Cut a small hole with sharp scissors. Then, poke the inside of the hole to firm up the opening. Insert the nose with glue, then wipe up any excess glue that might have leaked out before it dries.

Pro-tip: Alternatively, you can use a polymer clay nose just like you made for Isabelle. If you have any extra noses from the Isabelle project, feel free to use them here: just make sure that the proportions line up. Do not forget to add glass varnish to make the nose nice and shiny. We would not want to see a teddy bear with a dull looking nose!

21. Grab more curly wool to add dimension to the cheeks. Use layers here and start out small. Add layers as you see fit. Use a thin felting needle to ensure a smooth addition. Follow the natural curve of the head from the mouth to the eyes. Add to your desired fluffiness and make sure both sides are of equal fluff.

Pro-tip: You can grab some acrylic paint to add some color and dimension to your teddy bear figure. Use a darker brown color to fill in the inside of the ear, around the eyes, and on the top of the nose. Alternatively, you can do this same technique with very thin pieces of darker brown wool, but this step is optional.

22. At last, take a pinch of very thin black wool and needle felt the shape of the mouth. Begin at the bottom of the plastic nose and create a natural fish hook shape along the muzzle. It is very important to use a very thin strand of black wool and to use a thin felting needle. Remember: you can add wool but you cannot take it away!

23. Now grab the hands and legs that you made earlier.

24. Take the curly wool and wrap it evenly around the shapes. Make sure that you cover well and evenly just as you did for the head and body. Cover all of the hands and legs. Make sure that the hands and legs match up appropriately.

25. Next, attach the hands to the body. Seal it and secure it using more of the curly wool. Make sure to add a layer of wool all around the attachment to fill in any gaps. Layer multiple times and felt to blend and smooth.

26. Attach the legs. This teddy bear figure is in a sitting down position: attach the legs to the side of the torso so that it can sit down properly. Attach in the same way that you just did the hands. Use layers of curly wool to seal and secure. Layer multiple times to ensure a secure attachment and felt to blend and smooth with each layer. During this step, it is also nice to extend the extra curly fur around onto the back of the body. This will help create a nice and round bottom for your teddy bear to relax on.

27. Layer more wool to fill out the inner thigh.

28. Grab some more curly wool to add more volume to the belly. We do not want any scrawny teddies here! In this stage, it is helpful to pull the curly wool apart slightly to create a really fluffy texture to felt onto your teddy bear's body.

29. Finally, tie a red bow around your teddy bear's neck to give it some adorable style! A thin ribbon of your choice works great for this final touch.

Your teddy bear is ready for cuddling!

Pro-tip:

As I mentioned before, you can make this teddy bear project any size your heart desires! Of course, tiny teddies are extremely adorable in my humble opinion. Like with other projects, an easy way to elevate this project is to make little accessories for it. We made a bow in the above tutorial that went around the teddy bear's neck. You can make a bow for the head for an easy variation, or consider making a scarf in a fun or funky color. A sweater is also a great way to add some extra cute touches to this project.

Of course, another very easy way to change up this project is to choose different colors. You can create more realistic creatures by mimicking the natural colorations of bears in the wild—think black bears, polar bears, or grizzly bears. This is a fun way to turn this project into a realistic creature.

If you are feeling that realistic styles are not quite what you are looking for in this project, consider making this teddy bear in fun and unnatural colors. The rainbow is open for any choice! Red, orange, yellow, green, blue, or violet: you decide! You can create these fun colors in a solid fur option or switch things up by creating a white belly and a colored body. This is a super cute way to make a truly dynamic little figure.

Chapter 16:

Mini Needle Felted Trees

What better project to end on than making decorative needle felted trees? Once you have the basic shape of this project done, you will have fun decorating and customizing your own trees.

This project might be last, but it is certainly not least! All of the skills you have learned up to this point will come into play with this craft. It also requires more materials than previous projects, so it is a great one to end on and leave you set up with different needles and supplies to use on future crafts. Get ready to create your miniature Christmas tree farm!

Materials Required

1. Multiple needles, needle holder, or needle felting pen

2. At least three 40 gauge felting needles, spiral or triangular

3. Beading needle and thread to match

4. Foam base

Large Christmas Tree Materials

1. Two lengths of green roving, 50 x 4 centimeters

2. One length of red roving, 25 x 2 centimeters

3. One meter of trace gold chain

4. Colorful assortment of 8 millimeter and 4 millimeter beads

This larger Christmas tree's finished size is 12 centimeters tall, with a 7 centimeter diameter at the base.

Medium Christmas Tree Materials

1. Two lengths of ivory or cream roving, 30 x 4 centimeters

2. One length of red roving, 20 x 2 centimeters

3. Twenty 4 millimeter red glass heart beads

4. One 10 millimeter red glass heart bead

This medium Christmas tree's finished size is 9 centimeters tall, with a 4.5 centimeter diameter at the base.

Small Christmas Tree Materials

1. Two lengths of green roving, 15 x 3 centimeters

2. One length of red roving, 15 x 1 centimeters

3. Forty red seed beads

This small Christmas tree's finished size is 6 centimeters tall, with a 4 centimeter diameter at the base.

Steps to Follow

For the Large Christmas Tree

1. Working on your foam mat, tease the fibers of one length of green wool roving out a little. Fold the roving over so that you have made a tall triangular shape.

2. Take the other length of green wool roving and fluff it into a ball. Insert this shape inside of the flat triangle. Make sure that you have positioned the roving so that the triangle has a fatter end that gradually tapers into a point like a carrot.

3. Pull the sides of the outer green wool roving around so that you can encase the filling.

4. Begin shaping a cone. When you are making the large Christmas tree, you can use three needles to help this step of the process go quickly.

5. Begin needle felting your layers of green wool roving together. Turn your Christmas tree as you work so that you will get a uniform roundness and texture all over the tree.

6. Cup your forefinger and thumb together to securely hold the wool in place as you shape the flat bottom. You can periodically press the bottom against a flat work surface or table to make sure you are getting it flat enough. Remember, you want these Christmas trees to be able to stand up on their own.

7. Squeeze the wool together at the top of the tree as you carefully use one needle to create a fine point. You can use a delicate needle to pull out a few fibers at a time, and continually shape them into a pointy tip with your fingers.

8. Continue felting your Christmas tree until it gets very firm. You can pause and stand your tree up on a flat surface to make sure it can stand on its own. If it starts to tilt, you can work on the bottom more to keep it even.

9. When your tree is firm and nicely formed, take thin layers of the green wool roving and layer a neat surface over the Christmas tree. This will give your tree a smooth, even finish. Start this finishing process with two needles, and as you work it to a more delicate state, you will finish with one.

10. Wrap the length of red wool (25 x 2 centimeters for the large tree, as different lengths are specified for the size of each different Christmas tree) around the bottom of the tree. Needle felt it into place to make a bright, decorative base for your tree. Tuck any spare wool underneath the tree bottom.

With this step, you can make your tree a little unique. If you do not like how far the red roving goes up on the tree, you can needle felt it to be a thinner border at the base of the tree.

11. Use straight pins to mark and measure where your decorative trimmings are going to be fixed.

12. Once you have everything mapped out, you can use loose stitches to attach the gold chain to the tree where you pinned it up.

13. Attach a special bead to the top of the tree. You can pick a slightly larger golden bead to be the centerpiece, or you can even pick a star-shaped bead. To make the bead stand tall like a tree topper, you can thread a short length of sturdy wire through the bead and down into the tip of the tree.

14. When you have positioned your beads, stitch them on with a beading needle. Add as many bead baubles necessary to make sure your Christmas tree conveys the festive spirit!

For the Medium Christmas Tree

1. Working on your foam mat, tease the fibers of one length of ivory or cream wool roving out a little. Fold the roving over so that you have made a tall triangular shape.

2. Take the other length of ivory or cream wool roving and fluff it into a ball. Insert this shape inside of the flat triangle. Make sure you have positioned the roving so that the triangle has a fatter end that gradually tapers into a point like a carrot.

3. Pull the sides of the outer ivory or cream wool roving around so that you can encase the filling.

4. Begin shaping a cone. When you are making the medium Christmas tree, you have less wool roving for the overall shape of the tree, so you will want to only use two needles. Since this is a smaller scale project, you will need to be more delicate with your needle felting process.

5. Begin needle felting your layers of ivory or cream wool roving together. Turn your Christmas tree as you work so that you will get a uniform roundness and texture all over the tree.

6. Cup your forefinger and thumb together to securely hold the wool in place as you shape the flat bottom. You can periodically press the bottom against a flat work surface or table to make sure that you are getting it flat enough. Remember, you want these Christmas trees to be able to stand up on their own.

7. Squeeze the wool together at the top of the tree as you carefully use one needle to create a fine point. You can use a delicate needle to pull out a few fibers at a time, and continually shape them into a pointy tip with your fingers.

8. Continue felting your Christmas tree until it gets very firm. You can pause and stand your tree up on a flat surface to make sure it can stand on its own. If it starts to tilt, you can work on the bottom more to keep it even.

9. When your tree is firm and nicely formed, take thin layers of the ivory or cream wool roving and layer a neat surface over the Christmas tree. This will give your tree a smooth, even finish. Start this finishing process with two needles, and as you work it to a more delicate state, you will finish with one.

10. Wrap the length of red wool (20 x 2 centimeters for this medium tree, as different lengths are specified for the size of each different Christmas tree) around the bottom of the tree. Needle felt it into place to make a bright, decorative base for your tree. Tuck any spare wool underneath the tree bottom.

With this step, you can make your tree a little unique. If you do not like how far the red roving goes up on the tree, you can needle felt it to be a thinner border at the base of the tree. You can make it look different than the larger Christmas tree, or you can make the red base look about the same across all three trees.

11. Use straight pins to mark and measure where your decorative trimmings are going to be fixed.

12. Attach the 10 millimeter glass heart bead to the top of the tree. You can thread a short length of sturdy wire through the bead and down into the tip of the tree so the bead will stand tall like a tree topper.

13. When you have positioned your red heart beads, stitch them on with a beading needle. Add as many bead baubles necessary to make sure your Christmas tree conveys the festive spirit!

For the Small Christmas Tree

1. Working on your foam mat, tease the fibers of one length of green wool roving out a little. Fold the roving over so that you have made a tall triangular shape.

2. Take the other length of green wool roving and fluff it into a ball. Insert this shape inside of the flat triangle. Make sure that you have positioned the roving so that the triangle has a fatter end that gradually tapers into a point like a carrot.

3. Pull the sides of the outer green wool roving around so that you can encase the filling.

4. Begin shaping a cone. When you are making the large Christmas tree, you can use three needles to help this step of the process go quickly.

5. Begin needle felting your layers of green wool roving together. Turn your Christmas tree as you work so that you will get a uniform roundness and texture all over the tree.

6. Cup your forefinger and thumb together to securely hold the wool in place as you shape the flat bottom. You can periodically press the bottom against a flat work surface or table to make sure you are getting it flat enough. Remember, you want these Christmas trees to be able to stand up on their own.

7. Squeeze the wool together at the top of the tree as you carefully use one needle to create a fine point. You can use a delicate needle to pull out a few fibers at a time, and continually shape them into a pointy tip with your fingers.

8. Continue felting your Christmas tree until it gets very firm. You can pause and stand your tree up on a flat surface to make sure it can stand on its own. If it starts to tilt, you can work on the bottom more to keep it even.

9. When your tree is firm and nicely formed, take thin layers of the green wool roving and layer a neat surface over the Christmas tree. This will give your tree a smooth, even finish. Start this finishing process with two needles, and as you work it to a more delicate state, you will finish with one.

10. Wrap the length of red wool (15 x 1 centimeters for the small tree, as different lengths are specified for the size of each different Christmas tree) around the bottom of the tree. Needle felt it into place to make a bright, decorative base for your tree. Tuck any spare wool underneath the tree bottom.

With this step, you can make your tree a little unique. If you do not like how far the red roving goes up on the tree, you can needle felt it so that you have a thinner border at the base of the tree. You can make it look different than the large and medium Christmas trees, or you can make the red base look about the same on all three trees.

11. Use straight pins to mark and measure where your decorative trimmings are going to be fixed.

12. Attach a special bead to the top of the tree. You can pick a slightly larger bead to be the centerpiece, or you can even pick a star-shaped bead. To make the bead stand tall like a tree

topper, you can thread a short length of sturdy wire through the bead and down into the tip of the tree.

13. When you have positioned your red seed beads beads, stitch them on with a beading needle. Add as many bead baubles necessary to make sure your Christmas tree conveys the festive spirit!

Your needle felted trees are ready! This trio of trees will make an adorable centerpiece for your holiday meals. If you do not have room on the table, consider putting them on the mantel or a side table so all of your guests can "ooh" and "ahh" over the cuteness as they enter your winter wonderland.

Conclusion

Now that you have learned the basics of needle felting, you will be well on your way to developing your own patterns and products.

Needle felting is a therapeutic craft, mostly due to the repetitive motions of working the needle into the fibers. It has recently grown in popularity, rivaling the coloring book trend of a few years ago.

Needle felting is a great task you can do to destress. You can work the fibers into felt while watching a TV show or movie, and working them into a sculpture only takes a little more focus.

To get ideas on needle felting crafts you can make, just look around! Have you been wanting some new decorations for your house? Now you can needle felt your own! Make ornaments or garland like those you have learned while working through this book. Use needle felt writing to create a beautiful quote to hang on your wall. You added needle felt writing onto a pillowcase in Chapter 8, which you can definitely do again, but why not try your hand at needle felting an entire pillow? You can even needle felt a cute little set of teacups to display in your kitchen!

Think about the kind of jewelry you like to wear, or what you would give as gifts. If any of your friends wear dangly earrings, you can use the felted ball earrings pattern from this book to make pairs for them. You can also use the felted balls to make bracelets and statement necklaces.

The needle felted cherry bag charms is also a great jumping off point to make more needle felted fruits. You can make the fruits miniature so they can dangle from key rings, or you can make them bigger—or even to scale!—and display them as decorative sculptures. If you like the idea of key rings and bag charms, you are not limited to fruits—you can design colorful balls, or go back to the first project you ever did and make flat needle felted shapes to hang from key rings.

Everyone loves adorable needle felted animals, and you learned how to make a few in this book. If you want to try making other needle felted animals, think of your favorite critters. Do you love your puppy or kitty more than anything in the world? Try to make a needle felted version of them. You can make needle felted versions of family pets for your friends as well, or even open yourself up for commissions.

If you are interested in taking commissions, selling your own products, or even if you just want to see what other people are making, Etsy is the place to go. Many fiber artists are selling their wares on Etsy, so it is a great place to find inspiration. If you need patterns, a lot of artists sell them. You can also look around at various crafters' and fiber artists' blogs for inspiration and free tutorials.

Tips to Take Away

After doing the projects in this book, you are well on your way to being an advanced needle felter! For quick reference, here are the top five tips to remember as you continue your crafting work.

1. Keep Your Needle Straight

Whether you are using a standard notched needle, triangle needle, star needle, twisted needle, or reverse needle, you will want to keep it straight. Whatever angle you insert the needle into the wool fibers, you need to pull it back out in that same way. If you poke the needle into the fibers and try to pull it out as hard as you can, you might break off the tip of your needle.

You also want to keep your needle straight while it is in the fibers. If you bend it slightly, it could break due to the tangles gripping the notches of the needle. For this reason, it is best to use a consistent up and down motion when needle felting.

2. Do Not Force It

If you try to insert the needle into your fibers and are not able to, do not keep pushing! It might break the tip of your needle. Being unable to poke your needle into a certain area of fibers might mean that the section is already completely felted. In that case, you can move on to another section. If you think the resistant area still needs more agitation, then you can use a needle with a smaller gauge to finish the delicate work.

3. Work Evenly

Moving the fibers around as you felt will keep your work even. You want to make sure that all areas are equally stiff so your final project will look cohesive and sturdy. Use your fingers to feel the texture of the fibers as you needle felt, but make sure you are always aware of where your fingers are in relation to your needles. You do not want to poke yourself with one of these notched needles!

4. Felt in Layers

Instead of starting with a large chunk of wool fibers and working hard to felt it all, start with smaller amounts. As you felt a small portion of wool, you can layer more raw fiber on top and work it into what you have already completed. Adding fibers in later will not be a problem if you remember to work evenly and rely on the wool's overall texture to let you know when all fibers are consistent.

5. Use a Base

Instead of using short fiber wool as a core for all of your projects, you can use foam or wire to form a base. Think about this step as you are planning your pattern so that you can save on wool. Using wire to form an animal's body will not only save your money and wool, but it will also cut down on the steps needed to complete the project.

If you are making stuffed animals instead of sculptures, you can use pillow stuffing at the center of your project to keep it cuddly. If you need something firmer but still soft, you can try quilt batting. The options are limitless, so use your imagination!

References

13 needle felting projects for beginners. (n.d.). Gathered. Retrieved November 5, 2020,
from
https://www.gathered.how/arts-crafts/13-needle-felting-projects-for-beginners/

Alexas_Fotos. (2016). Flower Felt Orange Greeting. In *Pixabay.*
https://pixabay.com/photos/flower-felt-orange-greeting-card-1593467/

Alicja. (2019). Felt Scroll Material. In *Pixabay.*
https://pixabay.com/photos/felt-scroll-material-web-colorful-4007361/

Ariyo, S. (2019). black lokai photo. In *Unsplash.*
https://unsplash.com/photos/zlROZagixXY

Art, S. F. (2017, February 16). *Sarafina Fiber Art: Using Wire in Needle Felting.*
Sarafina Fiber Art.
http://sarafinafiberartblog.blogspot.com/2017/02/using-wire-in-needle-felting.
html

dreamwalker9. (2016b). Teddy Bear Needle Felting. In *Pixabay.*

https://pixabay.com/photos/teddy-bear-needle-felting-toy-1767729/

Eleanor Stanwood. (2014, June 23). Martha's Vineyard Arts & Ideas.
http://www.mvartsandideas.com/2014/06/eleanor-stanwood/

Håland, J. (2018). two white sheep photo. In *Unsplash*.
https://unsplash.com/photos/jPZvbjknC4E

Hermann, S., & Richter, F. (2017). Marguerite Heart Wood. In *Pixabay*.
https://pixabay.com/photos/marguerite-heart-wood-ivy-blossom-2380664/

HeungSoon. (2018a). Leather Craft Needle Thread. In *Pixabay*.
https://pixabay.com/photos/leather-craft-needle-thread-sew-3556442/

How Needle Felting Began—Felting Fridays. (n.d.). Star Magnolias. Retrieved
November 9, 2020, from
https://starmagnolias.com/blogmain/2016/11/18/how-needle-felting-began-felti
ng-fridays

How to needle felt. (n.d.). WikiHow. Retrieved November 5, 2020, from
https://www.wikihow.com/Needle-Felt

How To Use Wire For Needle Felting—Plus Mini Tutorial. (n.d.).
Lincolnshirefenncraftsblog.com. Retrieved November 9, 2020, from

https://lincolnshirefenncraftsblog.com/2020/04/17/
how-to-use-wire-for-needle
-felting-plus-mini-tutorial/

Schrøder, N. (2018). person holding white fur textile photo. In *Unsplash*.
https://unsplash.com/photos/z2CnusvHDco

Stux. (2014). Sheep's Wool Sheep Wool-Felt. In *Pixabay*.
https://pixabay.com/photos/sheep-s-wool-sheep-wool-felt-533756/

Stux. (2018). Felt Balls Sheep's Wool Natural. In *Pixabay*.
https://pixabay.com/photos/felt-balls-sheep-s-wool-3319208/